VEGAN REV' Diet Smoothie

The Twenty-Two Vegan Challenge:
50 Healthy and Delicious Vegan Diet Smoothie to Help you Lose Weight and Look Amazing

By
Tom Smith

VEGAN REV' DEIT SMOOTHIE

Copyright © 2019 by: Tom Smith

ISBN-13: 978-1-950772-18-6
ISBN-10: 1-950772-18-7

All Rights Reserved. No part of this publication may be reproduced in any form or by any means, including scanning, photocopying, or otherwise without prior written permission of the copyright holder.

Disclaimer:

The information provided in this book is designed to provide helpful information on the subjects discussed. The publisher and author are not responsible for any specific health or allergy needs that may require medical supervision and are not liable for any damages or negative consequences from any treatment, action, application or preparation, to any person reading or following the information in this book.

VEGAN REV' DEIT SMOOTHIE

Table of Contents

INTRODUCTION: 5

THE 22 DAY VEGAN SMOOTHIE TO HELP TRANSFORM YOUR BODY, RESET YOUR HABIT, AND CHANGE YOUR LIFE 6

- Banana Bread Super Foods Smoothie 6
- Apple Pie Green Smoothie 8
- Sleepy Strawberry Cheesecake Smoothie 9
- Green Energy Smoothie 11
- Mint Chocolate Chip Smoothie 12
- Blushing Apple Smoothie 14
- Sleepy Blueberry Muffin Smoothie 15
- Sleepy Raspberry Lemon Poppy Seed Smoothie 16
- Energy Smoothies 18
- Blueberry peach flavor 19

INGREDIENTS: 19

- Sleepy Banana Muffin Smoothie 20
- Pumpkin Spice Smoothie 21
- Sleepy Chocolate Chip Cookie Dough Smoothie 22
- Classic Green Smoothie 23
- Caramel-like green smoothie 24
- Key Lime Pie Green Smoothie 25
- Ultra Green Smoothie 26
- Superwoman Green Smoothie 27
- Chocolate Covered Raspberry Green Smoothie 28
- Pumpkin Orange Cream Smoothie 29
- Raspberry Green Smoothie 30
- Red Rooster Smoothie 31
- Watermelon Smoothie Cooler 32
- Bombay Banana Smoothie 33
- Triple Threat Green Smoothie 34

Popeye Banana Smoothie 35
Can't Beet This Smoothie 36
Cherry Almond Smoothie 37
Pumpkin Chai Smoothie 38
Pearrific Green Smoothie 39
Berry Immunity Smoothie 40
5-Minute Vegan Breakfast Smoothie 41
Happy Digestion Smoothie 42
Green Tea Lime Pie Smoothie Bowl 43
Creamy Chocolate Hemp Smoothie for Two 45
Green Warrior Protein Smoothie 46
Velvety Butternut Cinnamon Date Smoothie 47
Pink Power Detox Smoothie 48
Creamy Pumpkin Pie Smoothie for Two 49
Neon Pink Smoothie Juice 50
Peanut Butter Bomb Smoothie 51
Tropical Raspberry Lime Zinger 53
Tropical Mango Banana Popsicles 54
Easy Berry Parfaits 55
Chocolate Raspberry Smoothie 56
Creamy Holly Nog Smoothie 57
Pumpkin Gingerbread Smoothie 58
Chocolate Cake Batter Smoothie 59
Peppermint Patty Green Monster 60
Carrot Cake Smoothie 61

CONCLUSION 62

INTRODUCTION:

THE 22 DAY VEGAN CHALLENGE: TRANSFORM YOUR BODY, RESET YOUR HABIT, AND CHANGE YOUR LIFE

The vegan revolution is a groundbreaking program designed to transform your mental, emotional, and physical health in just 22 days.

The 22-Day vegan Revolution is founded on the principle that it takes 21 days to make or break a habit. *It* is also a plant-based diet designed to create lifelong habits that will empower you to live healthier, lose weight, or to reverse serious health issues. it benefits of a vegan diet are immense, most of which are: help prevent cancer, lower cholesterol levels, reduce the risk of heart disease, decrease blood pressure, and even reverse diabetes.

Marco Borges one of today's most sought-after health experts, exercise physiologist has spent years helping his exclusive list of high-profile clients to permanently change their lifestyle and bodies through his 22 day vegan revolution. Celebrities whose life has been touch with Marco Borges recent innovation ranges from Beyoncé, Jay-Z, Jennifer Lopez, and Pharrell Williams, to Gloria Estefan, and Shakira which have all turned to him for his expertise.

Diet and exercise are the building blocks for a healthy life, and Tom Smith when writing this book understands not only the scientific benefits to the human body, but also how to present the information in a way that is accessible, manageable, and inspirational. However, a plant-based diet can and will change your lifestyle for good. In *The vegan revolution diet smoothie* will show you the best vegan smoothies for a trim waistline, a strong heart, and a healthy brain.

However, the 22 Days Nutrition is founded on the ground that vegan meals are the healthiest meals you can eat. Vegan meals are known to be low in calories and packed with vitamins and nutrients that are essential to the body. So while taking the 22 Days Nutrition diet, expect to eat between 1200 to 2000 calories per day even when you're eating regular meals and snacks. Vegan food is exceptionally low in calories.

Finally, this book contains "healthy and delicious" vegan smoothies that anyone can use to break their bad dietary habits and start living a healthier life.

THE 22 DAY VEGAN SMOOTHIE TO HELP TRANSFORM YOUR BODY, RESET YOUR HABIT, AND CHANGE YOUR LIFE

Banana Bread Super Foods Smoothie

Tips:

Remember, this that vegan smoothie packed with super foods to help you reach your maximum health potential!

Ingredients

2 banana (frozen)

2 tablespoons of raw walnuts (or preferably hemp seeds)

2 medjool date (pitted)

1 ½ teaspoons of ground cinnamon

Extra walnuts and ground cinnamon (for topping)

2 cups of water

2/3 cup of cooked quinoa (or preferably buckwheat)

4 teaspoons of cold-pressed flax oil

Flesh from 2 vanilla bean or preferably 1 teaspoon alcohol-free pure vanilla extract

Pinch allspice

Directions:

1. First, you place in your blender in the order of the ingredients listed.
2. After that, you blend for 30 seconds or until smooth.
3. Then you pour into a glass and top with additional walnuts and ground cinnamon.

Nutrition Information

Per Serving

Calories: 354

VEGAN REV' DEIT SMOOTHIE

Total Fat: 16

Carbs: 53 g

Dietary Fiber: 6.9 g

Sugars: 23.8 g

Protein: 5.9 g

Apple Pie Green Smoothie

Ingredients

1 cup of unsweetened unpasteurized apple juice

1 teaspoon of ground cinnamon

Pinch of ground nutmeg

4 cups of spinach

1 cup of water

2 tablespoons of walnuts

½ teaspoon of vanilla extract (or preferably maple extract)

1 English cucumber

2 apple (chopped and frozen)

½ avocado (chopped and frozen)

4-6 ice cubes

Directions:

1. First, you place the entire ingredients in your blender.
2. After that, you blend for 30 seconds or until smooth.

Nutrition Information

Per Serving

Calories: 314

Total Fat: 12.8

Carbs: 50.8 g

Dietary Fiber: 10.8 g

Sugars: 34.6 g

Protein: 5.7 g

Sleepy Strawberry Cheesecake Smoothie

Ingredients

2 cups of non-dairy milk (I prefer unsweetened almond milk)

2 tablespoons of chia seed

2 teaspoons of apple cider vinegar

Pinch stevia

2 cups of strawberries

6 tablespoons of uncontaminated oats

2 tablespoons of cashews

2 teaspoons of lemon juice

1 teaspoon of vanilla

Directions:

Tips:

Remember, if you want it to be made the night before you plan on eating it, or at least 4 hours in advance.

1. First, you combine all ingredients in a glass container [preferably a mason jars and give it a quick shake].
2. After which you place in the fridge overnight.
3. Furthermore, in the morning, you pour ingredients into blender and process until smooth.
4. Then you top with cashews and strawberries.

Nutrition Information

Per Serving

Calories: 224

Total Fat: 10

Carbs: 28.4 g

VEGAN REV' DEIT SMOOTHIE

Dietary Fiber: 7.3 g

Sugars: 8.8 g

Protein: 6.9 g

Green Energy Smoothie

Ingredients

6 cups of raw spinach

2 cups of organic green tea

1 inch of fresh ginger root

2 cucumber (seeded and sliced)

4 cups of honeydew melon (cubed about 1 medium sized melon)

2 teaspoons of lemon juice

Directions:

1. First, you place the entire ingredient in the blender and blend.
2. Enjoy

Nutrition Information

Per Serving

Calories: 67

Total Fat: 0.7

Carbs: 14.3 g

Dietary Fiber: 3.5 g

Sugars: 8 g

Protein: 4.6 g

Mint Chocolate Chip Smoothie

NOTE:

If you want to boost the detoxifying and cleansing properties of this smoothie, I suggest you add chlorella or spirulina powder!

Ingredients

4 cups of spinach

6 tablespoons of non-diary chocolate chips (divided)

1 cup of non-dairy milk (I prefer unsweetened rice milk)

12 ice cubes

2 peppermint tea bag

4 tablespoons of hemp hearts

1 cup of boiling water

2 medium frozen banana

Directions:

Tips:

If you want to be prepared at least 30 minutes in advance:

1. First, you steep the tea in the 1 cup boiling water until ready to use in the smoothie so that it's really concentrated.
2. After that, you wait until the water has cooled, about 30 minutes (for me I just make my tea at night and let it sit on the counter overnight).
3. At this point, you place all ingredients but chocolate chips in your blender.
4. After which you blend for 30 seconds or until smooth.
5. Then you drop in half of the chocolate chips and pulse quickly.
6. Finally, you pour into a cup and top with leftover chocolate.

Nutrition Information

Per Serving

Calories: 329

VEGAN REV' DEIT SMOOTHIE

Total Fat: 10.6

Carbs: 52.1 g

Dietary Fiber: 7.1 g

Sugars: 26.9 g

Blushing Apple Smoothie

Ingredients

1 English cucumber

1 cup of fresh raspberries

12-16 ice cubes

1 cup of pitted fresh cherries

2 apple

2 tablespoons of chia seed

1 cup of water

Directions:

1. First, you place in your blender in the order of the ingredients listed.
2. After that, you blend for 30 seconds or until smooth.

Nutrition Information

Per Serving

Calories: 175

Total Fat: 3

Carbs: 37.9 g

Dietary Fiber: 7.4 g

Sugars: 12.1 g

Protein: 2.8 g

Sleepy Blueberry Muffin Smoothie

Ingredients

1 cup of blueberries

2 teaspoons of pure vanilla extract

2 tablespoons of chia seed

3 cups of non-dairy milk

4 tablespoons of uncontaminated regular oats (preferably feel free to use packaged gluten free oatmeal, gluten free granola, or quinoa flakes)

2 tablespoons of vanilla protein powder

Directions:

Tips: if you want it to be made the night before you plan on eating it, or at least 4 hours in advance

<u>**In the Night before**</u>:

1. First, you combine all ingredients (but the blueberries) in a glass or plastic container.
2. After which you stir to combine and place in fridge.
3. After that, In the Morning you pour contents of container into blender, add blueberries and blend until smooth.

Nutrition Information

 Per Serving

Calories: 256

Total Fat: 7.5

Carbs: 13.5 g

Dietary Fiber: 7 g

Sugars: 0.9 g

Protein: 31.9 g

Sleepy Raspberry Lemon Poppy Seed Smoothie

Ingredients

1 cup of raspberries

2 tablespoons of lemon juice

2 tablespoons of chia seeds

2 teaspoons of pure vanilla extract

Pinch white stevia powder

3 cups of non-dairy milk

4 tablespoons of uncontaminated rolled oats

2 tablespoons of almond butter

3 teaspoons of poppy seeds

Zest from 2 small lemons

Ingredients for the Toppings

Raspberries and lemon

Directions: Tips:

If you want it to be made the night before you plan on eating it, or at least 4 hours in advance.

1. First, you combine all ingredients in a glass container [preferably mason jars and give it a quick shake].
2. After which you place in the fridge overnight.
3. Then in the morning, you pour ingredients into blender and process until smooth.

Nutrition Information

Per Serving

Calories: 266

Total Fat: 18.1

Carbs: 20 g

VEGAN REV' DEIT SMOOTHIE

Dietary Fiber: 9.6 g

Sugars: 4.2 g

Protein: 8.8

Energy Smoothies

Notes:

1. Feel free to make this smoothie right in the blender, or have it sit overnight (I prefer letting it sit overnight so the chia has time to get really gelatinous).
2. Remember, if you don't want to use green tea because of the caffeine, try a nice herbal tea.

Ingredients

Strawberry banana flavor

12 strawberries

2 scoops of protein powder

2 serving probiotics

1 banana

2 cups of green tea

2 tablespoons of chia seeds

Blueberry peach flavor

INGREDIENTS:

2 cups of blueberries

2 scoops of protein powder

2 serving probiotics

1 peach

2 cups of green tea

2 tablespoons of chia seeds

Directions:

1. First, you choose a flavor, or prepare both.
2. Remember they stay well in the fridge for 2 days, so I suggest you make both ahead of time.
3. After which you combine all ingredients in a 1L mason jar.
4. After that, you seal and place in the fridge overnight.
5. Then in the morning, you place contents in a blender and blend to your heart's content.
6. Enjoy!

Nutrition Information

Per Serving

Calories: 257

Total Fat: 6.7

Carbs: 27.9 g

Dietary Fiber: 7.5 g

Sugars: 14.1 g

Protein: 25.1 g

Sleepy Banana Muffin Smoothie

Ingredients

2 frozen banana

2 tablespoons of raisins

2 tablespoons of raw walnuts

2 cups of non-dairy milk (+ ½ cup for blending)

4 tablespoons of uncontaminated regular oats

1 teaspoon of pure vanilla extract

Pinch of ground cinnamon

Optional toppings: coconut, raisins, walnuts, or chocolate chips

Directions:

In the Night before:

1. First, you combine all ingredients [but the frozen banana and ½ cup of milk] in a glass or plastic container.
2. After which you stir to combine and place in fridge.
3. Then in the Morning, you pour contents of container into blender.
4. After that, you add banana and additional milk, blend until smooth.

Nutrition Information

Per Serving

Calories: 256

Total Fat: 8.2

Carbs: 43.3 g

Dietary Fiber: 6.1 g

Sugars: 20.3 g

Protein: 5.8 g

Pumpkin Spice Smoothie

Ingredients

1 cup of canned pumpkin

2 tablespoons of raisins (or preferably 1 teaspoon maple syrup)

½ teaspoon of ground cinnamon

Pinch of ground nutmeg

Vegan coconut whipped topping

2 cups of non-dairy milk

1 banana

1 teaspoon of pure vanilla extract

¼ teaspoon of ground ginger

Pinch of ground cloves

Pinch of all spice

Directions:

1. First, you place everything but whipped topping in the blender.
2. After which you blend until smooth
3. After that, you pour into your favorite glass and place a couple tablespoons of coconut whipped cream on top.
4. Then you sprinkle with cinnamon if you so wished.

Nutrition Information

Per Serving

Calories: 212

Total Fat: 10.4

Carbs: 29.5 g

Dietary Fiber: 7.2 g

Sugars: 14.6 g

Protein: 3.8 g

Sleepy Chocolate Chip Cookie Dough Smoothie

Ingredients

12 tablespoons of uncontaminated oats

2 tablespoons of almond butter

½ teaspoon of pure vanilla extract

2 cups of non-dairy milk + ½ cup for blending (I prefer unsweetened almond milk)

2 tablespoons of chia seeds

2 tablespoons of cacao powder

Directions:

1. If you want it to be made the night before you plan on eating it, or at least 4 hours in advance.
2. First, you combine all ingredients in a glass container [preferably the mason jars and give it a quick shake].
3. After which, you place in the fridge overnight.
4. Then in the morning, you pour ingredients into blender, add additional ½ cup milk, and process until smooth.
5. Finally, you top with cacao nibs + coconut

Nutrition Information

Per Serving

Calories: 244

Total Fat: 16.4

Carbs: 20.2 g

Dietary Fiber: 7.1 g

Sugars: 0.6 g

Protein: 9.1 g

Classic Green Smoothie

Ingredients

4 cups of organic spinach

4 tablespoons of ground flax seed

6 ice cubes

2 cups of unsweetened non-dairy milk

2 bananas (frozen)

2 tablespoons of raw almond butter

Directions:

1. First, you place in your blender in the order of the ingredients listed.
2. After that, you blend for 30 seconds or until smooth.

Nutrition Information

Per Serving

Calories: 330

Total Fat: 18.1

Carbs: 40.5 g

Dietary Fiber: 9 g

Sugars: 14.7 g

Protein: 9.4 g

Caramel-like green smoothie

Ingredients

2 apples (chopped and frozen)

4 cups of spinach

½ teaspoon of pure vanilla extract

4 ice cubes

2 cups of non-dairy milk

4 tablespoons of sun butter

4 medjool dates (pitted)

¼ teaspoon of ground cinnamon

Pinch of salt

Directions:

1. First, you place in your blender in the order of the ingredients listed.
2. Then you blend for 30 seconds or until smooth.

Nutrition Information

Per Serving

Calories: 505

Total Fat: 18.8

Carbs: 81.8 g

Dietary Fiber: 11 g

Sugars: 58.4 g

Protein: 10.9 g

Key Lime Pie Green Smoothie

Ingredients

2 teaspoons of key lime zest (about 4 limes)

2 ripe frozen banana

4 drops liquid stevia (or preferably 2 tablespoons of ground xylitol or 2 pitted medjool date)

4 cups of organic baby spinach

Gluten-free graham cracker pieces (it is optional)

4 tablespoons of key lime juice (about 8 limes)

2 cups of unsweetened non-dairy milk

½ teaspoon of alcohol-free vanilla extract

2 tablespoons of sunflower butter

8 ice cubes

1 minute vanilla whipped topping (it is optional)

Directions:

1. First, you place in your blender in the order of the ingredients listed.
2. After which you blend for 30 seconds or until smooth.

Nutrition Information

Per Serving

Calories: 293

Total Fat: 11.3

Carbs: 51 g

Dietary Fiber: 6.4 g

Sugars: 15.4 g

Protein: 7.4 g

Ultra Green Smoothie

Ingredients

4 cups of organic spinach

1 banana (frozen)

6 ice cubes

2 cups of unsweetened non-dairy milk

1 avocado (frozen)

4 tablespoons of hemp hearts (or better still hemp seeds)

Directions:

1. First, you place in your blender.
2. After which you blend for 30 seconds or until smooth.

Nutrition Information

Per Serving

Calories: 357

Total Fat: 24.2

Carbs: 29.2 g

Dietary Fiber: 12.6 g

Sugars: 8.1 g

Protein: 10.4 g

Superwoman Green Smoothie

Ingredients

2 cups of spinach

2 tablespoons of almond butter

2 tablespoons of unpasteurized honey

6-12 ice cubes

2 cups of unsweetened non-dairy milk

2 tablespoons of cacao powder

2 tablespoons of coconut oil

2 teaspoons of spirulina

2 cups of frozen mixed berries

Directions:

1. First, you place in your blender.
2. Then you blend for 30 seconds or until smooth.

Notes

1. Remember, if you're new to spirulina and not a big fan of the taste, I suggest you try adding two tablespoons of cacao powder to hide the taste.
2. After that, you slowly work your way up to one to two teaspoons of spirulina and one tablespoons of cacao.

Nutrition Information

Per Serving

Calories: 419

Total Fat: 27.9

Carbs: 43.8 g

Dietary Fiber: 8.9 g

Sugars: 27.5 g

Protein: 7.6 g

Chocolate Covered Raspberry Green Smoothie

Ingredients

4 cups of organic spinach

4 tablespoons of ground flax seed

2-6 ice cubes

2 cups of unsweetened non-dairy milk

2 cups of raspberries

4 tablespoons of shredded coconut

2 tablespoons of cacao powder

Directions:

1. First, you place in your blender.
2. Then you blend for 30 seconds or until smooth.

Nutrition Information

Per Serving

Calories: 240

Total Fat: 14.3

Carbs: 26.9 g

Dietary Fiber: 16.5 g

Sugars: 6.5 g

Protein: 8.1 g

Pumpkin Orange Cream Smoothie

Ingredients

1 cup of vanilla non-dairy yogurt

1 cup of unsweetened orange juice

2 tablespoons of freshly ground flax seed

½ teaspoon of ground cinnamon

Pinch ground cloves

2 medium orange (peeled and sliced)

1 cup of canned pumpkin puree

2 tablespoons of sweetener (like raisins, medjool dates, maple syrup, coconut nectar, etc.)

2 small knob ginger

Splash alcohol-free vanilla extract

Directions:

1. First, you place all ingredients in your blender.
2. Then you blend for 30 seconds or until smooth.

Nutrition Information

Per Serving

Calories: 347

Total Fat: 6.2

Carbs: 72.3 g

Dietary Fiber: 12.2 g

Sugars: 45.2 g

Protein: 9.4 g

Raspberry Green Smoothie

Ingredients

2 ripe pear (sliced with core removed)

2 cups of baby spinach

1 teaspoon of gluten-free pure vanilla extract

2 cups of non-dairy milk

2 cups of frozen raspberries

4 leaves kale

Directions:

1. First, you place all ingredients in your blender.
2. Then you blend for 30 seconds or until smooth.

Nutrition Information

Per Serving

Calories: 215

Total Fat: 4.1

Carbs: 45 g

Dietary Fiber: 15.3 g

Sugars: 19.2 g

Protein: 6.1 g

Red Rooster Smoothie

Note:

Have in mind that adding protein powder or chia seed into the mix will help with natural separation of the ingredients

Ingredients:

12 strawberries

30 green grapes

1 orange (skin removed)

8-12 ice cubes

1 cups of water

4 slices of raw red beet (chopped approx. 4 tablespoons)

1 cucumber (skin removed)

4 large handfuls of spinach

Directions:

1. First, you add all ingredients to the jug of your blender.
2. After which you blend for about 20-30 seconds, until smooth.
3. Then you serve immediately.

Watermelon Smoothie Cooler

Ingredients

1 cup of coconut water

4 cups of cubed watermelon

10 frozen strawberries

Directions:

First, you add all ingredients to your blender and blend until smooth.

Notes:
you can boost the smoothie by adding: protein powder, chia seeds, hemp seeds or flax seed before blending.

Nutrition Information

Per Serving

Calories: 150

Total Fat: 0.5

Carbs: 36.9 g

Dietary Fiber: 2 g

Sugars: 27.1 g

Protein: 2.3 g

Bombay Banana Smoothie

Ingredients:

2 medium banana

4 medjool dates, (pitted)

2 (yield about two teaspoons) knob of fresh ginger (skin removed)

2 cups of non-dairy milk (I prefer unsweetened almond milk)

2 teaspoons of creamed coconut (or preferably coconut butter)

1 teaspoon of chai spice (also known as chai or better still tea masala)

Directions:

1. First, you place all the ingredients in your blender.
2. Then you blend for 30 seconds or until smooth.

Nutrition Information

Per Serving

Calories: 298

Total Fat: 6.6

Carbs: 61.4 g

Dietary Fiber: 8.1 g

Sugars: 40.5 g

Protein: 4.2 g

Triple Threat Green Smoothie

Ingredients:

2 cups of cubed honeydew melon

40 green grapes, optional (to add sweetness)

6-8 ice cubes

20 ounces brewed green tea, cooled (better still you could also just use water)

2 plum (pitted)

1 cucumber (skin removed and chopped)

2 large handful of spinach

Directions:

1. First, you add all ingredients to the jug of your blender.
2. After which you blend for about 20-30 seconds, until smooth.
3. Then you serve immediately.

Notes

1. Remember that adding protein powder or chia will help with separation.
2. For me I don't mind the separation (I swish the mixture around and it goes away!) but it's a preference thing.

Nutrition Information

Per Serving

Calories: 127

Total Fat: 0.6

Carbs: 31.2 g

Dietary Fiber: 5 g

Sugars: 20.8 g

Protein: 3.2 g

Popeye Banana Smoothie

Ingredients

1 cup of vanilla goat dairy yogurt (or preferably non-dairy yogurt)

4 handfuls of fresh spinach

½ teaspoon of almond extract

1 cup of water

1 banana

2 tablespoons of raw almonds

Directions:

1. First, you place all the ingredients in your blender.
2. Then you blend for 30 seconds or until smooth.
3. Enjoy!

Nutrition Information

Per Serving

Calories: 191

Total Fat: 4.9

Carbs: 25.7 g

Dietary Fiber: 3.6 g

Sugars: 16.4 g

Protein: 10.6 g

Can't Beet This Smoothie

Ingredients

2 large beet juiced (about 6 tablespoons)

1 banana

4 apples, juiced (about 1 1/3 cups of apple juice)

2 cups of mixed frozen berries

Directions:

1. First you place all ingredients in your blender.
2. Then you blend for about 30 seconds or until smooth.

Nutrition Information

Per Serving

Calories: 237

Total Fat: 1.1

Carbs: 58.5 g

Dietary Fiber: 6.7 g

Sugars: 43.3 g

Protein: 2.4 g

Cherry Almond Smoothie

Ingredients

2 scoop vanilla protein powder

2 teaspoons pure almond extract

1 teaspoon camu camu powder a powerful super food with lots of anti-inflammatory and anti-oxidant properties (it is optional)

1 teaspoon guar gum to enhance creaminess (it is optional)

2 cups of pitted cherries (fresh or frozen)

4 teaspoons of almond butter

1 teaspoon of maca root powder (it is optional and doesn't affect the taste or texture)

2 cups of water (or preferably unsweetened almond milk)

12-16 ice cubes ice

Directions:

1. First, you place all ingredients in a blender except for the ice and guar gum.
2. After which you blend until almost smooth.
3. After that you add ice and guar gum, and continue blending.
4. Then you pour into glasses and enjoy!

Nutrition Information

Per Serving

Calories: 257

Total Fat: 8.8

Carbs: 21.8 g

Dietary Fiber: 3 g

Sugars: 15.1 g

Protein: 25.4 g

Pumpkin Chai Smoothie

Ingredients:

1 cup of canned (or preferably fresh pureed pumpkin)

2 tablespoons of chia seeds

2 knob of fresh ginger

8 ice cubes

3 cup non-dairy milk (I prefer unsweetened almond milk)

2 medium banana (frozen)

4 medjool dates (pitted)

3 teaspoons of homemade chai spice

1 teaspoon of pure gluten-free vanilla extract

Directions:

1. First, you place all ingredients in your blender.
2. Then you blend for about 30 seconds or until smooth.

Nutrition Information

Per Serving

Calories: 418

Calories from Fat: 130

Total Fat: 14.5

Carbs: 65.4 g

Dietary Fiber: 20.4 g

Sugars: 31.3 g

Protein: 10.8 g

Pearrific Green Smoothie

Ingredients

4 celery sticks

2 small knob ginger

4 cups of spinach

12-16 ice cubes

4 kale leaves

4 carrots

2 pear (core removed and sliced)

2 tablespoons of chia seeds

Directions:

Note: if you have a 'low' setting on your juicer, I suggest you begin with the softer items first – kale.

1. After which you turn to 'high' and juice the celery, carrots and ginger.
2. After that, you place fresh juice in the blender with spinach, pear slices, chia seeds and ice cubes.
3. Then blend until smooth, for about 30 seconds.

Nutrition Information

Per Serving

Calories: 258

Total Fat: 6

Carbs: 47.8 g

Dietary Fiber: 11.8 g

Sugars: 19.9 g

Protein: 8.7 g

Berry Immunity Smoothie

Ingredients

1 fresh or possibly frozen banana

4 tablespoons of unsweetened cranberry sauce

1 cup of fresh or preferably frozen blueberries

2 tablespoons of chia seed, flax seed or hemp seed

1 cup of tightly packed kale leaves

1 cup of homemade apple juice

Directions:

1. First you place all ingredients in your blender.
2. After which you blend for about 30 seconds or until smooth.

Nutrition Information

Per Serving

Calories: 227

Total Fat: 5.8

Carbs: 48 g

Dietary Fiber: 9.6 g

Sugars: 27.3 g

Protein: 5.4 g

5-Minute Vegan Breakfast Smoothie

Ingredients:

2 ripe banana (sliced)

2 tablespoons of coconut oil

2 teaspoons of powdered ginger

2 cups of almond milk

2 cups of frozen fruit medley (favorite: strawberry, mango, pineapple, papaya)

2-4 tablespoons of chia seeds

Directions:

1. First, you combine the almond milk, frozen fruit, banana, coconut oil, chia seeds, and powdered ginger in a blender and purée until smooth.
2. Then you pour into a glass and serve immediately.

Notes

Remember, if you have fresh ginger on hand, I suggest you substitute the powdered with a half teaspoon of grated ginger root.

NUTRITIONAL FACT

Per serving, based on 1 servings. (% daily value)

Calories: 309

Fat: 20.6 g (31.6%)

Carbs: 29.3 g (9.8%)

Fiber: 7.5 g (29.8%)

Sugars: 20.9 g

Protein: 4.8 g (9.7%)

Happy Digestion Smoothie

Ingredients:

1 frozen banana

1 cup of coconut water

4 tablespoons of avocado

Lemon slice (for garnish)

2 heaping cup frozen pineapple chunks (or preferably fresh, if desired)

1 cup of water

½ cup of packed fresh parsley

2 teaspoons of packed freshly grated ginger

½ teaspoon of probiotic powder (it is optional)

Directions:

1. First, you add all ingredients into a blender.
2. After that, you blend on the highest speed until super smooth.

Tips:

1. Feel free to add a handful of baby spinach, if you wish.
2. Remember that fresh mint would also give this smoothie a nice digestion boost!

Green Tea Lime Pie Smoothie Bowl

Ingredients:

Ingredients For the smoothie:

2 cups of fresh baby spinach

Packed ½ cup of avocado

2 tablespoons + 2 teaspoons of fresh lime juice

½ teaspoon of Matcha green tea powder (it is optional)

1 ½ cups of coconut water

2 large frozen banana

4 teaspoons of lime zest

4 ice cubes

2-4 teaspoons of pure maple syrup, to taste

Topping ideas:

Melted coconut butter

Matcha green tea powder

Hemp hearts

Granola

Large flake dried coconut

Lime zest

Directions:
1. First, you add all the smoothie ingredients into a high speed blender.
2. After which you blend on high until smooth.

VEGAN REV' DEIT SMOOTHIE

3. After that, you adjust sweetness if desired.
4. Then you pour into a bowl and sprinkle on the toppings of your choice.
5. Feel free to enjoy with a spoon!

Tips:

Remember that it is easiest to zest the lime *before* juicing.

Creamy Chocolate Hemp Smoothie for Two

Ingredients:

4-6 pitted large Medjool dates, to taste

6 tablespoons of hulled hemp seed

8 large ice cubes

4 cups of almond milk

6 tablespoons of unsweetened Dutch-processed cocoa powder

2 large peeled and frozen banana

½ teaspoon of cinnamon

Directions:

1. First, you add all ingredients into a high-speed blender.
2. After which you blend until super smooth.

Tip:

Note that this recipe yields a fairly thin consistency.

1. If you want a thicker shake-like texture, I suggest you try reducing the milk to 3.5 cups instead of 4 cups or go wild and add a scoop of your favorite non-dairy ice cream.
2. In the other hand, if your dates are a bit firm or dry, soak them in water for about 30-60 minutes before making this smoothie.
3. Feel free to swap the dates for liquid sweetener if desired (all you do is to just reduce the almond milk a bit so it's not too thin).

Green Warrior Protein Smoothie

Ingredients:

2 cups of destemmed dinosaur/lacinato kale

2 cups of chopped cucumber

6-8 tablespoons of hemp hearts (I use 8 tablespoons)

¼ cup of fresh mint leaves

1-2 tablespoons of algae oil (do not add to smoothie - take separately), optional

1 cup of fresh red grapefruit juice

2 large sweet apple (cored and roughly chopped)

Heaping 1 cup of chopped celery (2 med. stalk)

½ cup of frozen mango

1 tablespoon of virgin coconut oil (it is optional)

6-8 ice cubes (as needed)

Directions:
1. First, you juice half of a large red grapefruit.
2. After which you add 1 cup grapefruit juice to the blender.
3. After that, you add the kale, celery, apple, cucumber, mint, coconut oil, hulled hemp seeds, mango, and ice.
4. Then you blend on high until super smooth. (If you using a Vitamix, I suggest you use the tamper stick to push it down until it blends). Feel free to add a bit of water if necessary to get it blending.
5. At this point, you pour into a glass and enjoy immediately!

Velvety Butternut Cinnamon Date Smoothie

Ingredients:

2 cups + ½ cup (packed) roasted butternut squash or better still 1 ½ -2 cups of canned puréed squash

2 tablespoons of chia seeds

3 teaspoons of pure vanilla extract

10-12 large ice cubes (or as needed)

2 cups + 1 cup of almond milk

6-8 large Medjool dates (pitted)

2-4 teaspoons of cinnamon, to taste

1 teaspoon of ground ginger

Sprinkle of ground cloves

Directions:

Directions if you want to cook the squash:

1. Meanwhile, you heat oven to a temperature of 400F and line a baking sheet with parchment paper.
2. After which you slice the stem off the squash (it is optional) and slice the squash in half lengthwise.
3. After that, you scoop out the seeds with a spoon.
4. Then you brush a bit of oil on the squash and sprinkle with a pinch of salt.
5. Furthermore, you place squash on the baking sheet, cut side up, and roast for about 35-50 minutes, until fork tender and golden brown on the bottom.
6. Finally, you allow to cool.

Direction For the smoothie:

1. First, you add all smoothie ingredients into a high speed blender.
2. After which you blend on high until smooth, adjusting the spices as needed.
3. Then you serve immediately and enjoy!

Note:

If you want to make this nut-free, I suggest you use a nut-free non-dairy milk such as coconut or soy milk.

Pink Power Detox Smoothie

Ingredients:

1 medium avocado (pitted)

2 cups of strawberries (frozen preferred), hulled if necessary

2 lemon, juiced (about 6 tablespoons or so)

2 apples, if sweeter smoothie is desired (it is optional), cored and roughly chopped

2 cups of water (or better still coconut water)

4 celery stalks (roughly chopped)

2 small/medium beet (ends trimmed and roughly chopped)

2 tablespoons of coconut oil

8 large ice cubes

Directions:

1. First, you steam beet if necessary before starting.
2. After which you add all ingredients into a high-speed blender and blend on high until smooth.
3. Then you adjust sweetness if desired, this you do by adding an apple or liquid sweetener to taste if needed.

Creamy Pumpkin Pie Smoothie for Two

Ingredients:

1 cup of rolled oats

2 cups of canned pumpkin

2 frozen ripe banana

1 teaspoon of ground ginger

Coconut Whipped Cream, for garnish

4 cups of almond milk

4 tablespoons of chia seeds

1 tablespoon of blackstrap molasses

4 teaspoons of cinnamon

½ teaspoon of ground nutmeg

3-4 tablespoons of pure maple syrup

Directions:

1. First, you whisk together the milk, oats, and chia seeds in a medium-sized bowl.
2. After which you place in fridge for 1 hour or preferably overnight.
3. After that, you add soaked oat mixture to blender along with the molasses, pumpkin, frozen banana, and spices.
4. At this point, you blend until smooth.
5. Then you add about 5 ice cubes and blend until ice cold.
6. In addition, you add maple syrup to taste (I found 3 tablespoons perfect for me)
7. Finally, you serve with Coconut Whipped Cream and a sprinkle of cinnamon on top!

Neon Pink Smoothie Juice

Ingredients:

1 small raw beet (peeled and roughly chopped)

Fresh Grapefruit juice, to taste (I prefer 12 tablespoons of fresh grapefruit juice) or other citrus to taste

1 English cucumber (peeled and roughly chopped)

2 apple (cored and roughly chopped)

6-10 ice cubes

Directions:

1. First, you add the cucumber in a high-speed blender and blend on low speed to break it up.
2. After which you add the beet and apple.
3. After that, you blend, starting on a lower speed, and gradually increase the speed (I prefer my Vitamix plunger stick a lot to push it down and stir it as it was coming together. If desired, add a bit of water).
4. At this point, you blend on highest speed for about 1-2 minutes.
5. Then add in citrus juice to taste and about 4 ice cubes.
6. Furthermore, you blend again until smooth.
7. Make sure you serve immediately.

Peanut Butter Bomb Smoothie

Ingredients for the smoothies:

4 large frozen ripe bananas

6 tablespoons of natural peanut butter

Peanut butter crunch balls (crumbled on top)

4 cups of almond milk

2 tablespoons of chia seeds

½ teaspoon of pure vanilla extract

Ice (if desired)

***Ingredients for the peanut butter crunch balls*: (yield: 38-40 mini bites)**

2 cups of rolled oats, ground into flour (or preferably 2 cup + 4 tablespoons of oat flour)

2 tablespoons of packed brown sugar

½ teaspoon of fine grain sea salt

6 tablespoons of natural peanut butter

4 tablespoons of pure maple syrup

2 tablespoons of almond milk

½ teaspoon of pure vanilla extract

½ cup of rice crisp cereal

Directions:

a. First, you grind the rolled oats into a flour or just use oat flour in the blender.
2. After which you process together the ingredients for the crunch balls in a food processor (except for the rice crisp cereal).
3. After that, you adjust to taste.
NOTE: If batter is dry, I suggest you add a touch more liquid.
4. Then you stir in the cereal and form into tiny balls (I made about 19).

VEGAN REV' DEIT SMOOTHIE

5. Make sure you store leftovers in freezer.
6. Secondly, you add the smoothie ingredients, except for the crunch balls in a blender.
7. After which you blend until smooth (add ice if desired).
8. After that, you pour into two glasses and top with crumbled crunch balls.
9. Finally, you serve immediately with a spoon!

Tropical Raspberry Lime Zinger

Ingredients:

2 cups of frozen (or better still fresh raspberries)

4 tablespoons of fresh lime juice

Ice (if necessary)

2 cups of water

2 large frozen banana (make sure you peel and freeze before making)

2 teaspoons of coconut oil

2 teaspoons of agave, or to taste (or preferably other liquid sweetener)

Directions:

1. First, you add all ingredients into the blender and blend until smooth.
2. After which you adjust sweetness to taste.
   NOTE: You may need more or less agave depending on how tart your berries are.
3. Then you add ice if desired. Slurp.

Tropical Mango Banana Popsicles

Ingredients:

4 cups of frozen mango chunks

Splash of coconut extract (it is optional)

4 ripe bananas

1 cup of almond milk (or preferably coconut milk)

Directions:

First, you add all ingredients in a blender and blend until smooth.
Then you pour into Popsicle molds (or preferably ice cube trays) and freeze until set.

Easy Berry Parfaits

Ingredients:

2-3 cups of fresh mixed berries

Shredded coconut (to garnish)

4 large frozen (ripe bananas)

1 cup of Lightened up Summer Granola (or other granola)

Easy Chocolate sauce: you heat and whisk together: 2 teaspoon of coconut oil, 2 teaspoons of pure maple syrup, and 2 teaspoons of cocoa powder

Directions:

4. First, you peel and freeze your bananas until solid, preferably overnight.
5. After which you drop in the frozen banana chunks in a food processor and process until creamy and smooth.
6. After that, you stop and scrape down the sides of the bowl as necessary.
7. Feel free to give it a splash of almond milk to help it along (**NOTE**: Nut butter is also a nice add in too).
8. Then you add the banana soft serve, granola, and fresh fruit in layers in a couple glasses or parfait dishes.
9. Finally, you pour the chocolate sauce on top and serve immediately.

Chocolate Raspberry Smoothie

Ingredients:

1 ½ cup of frozen (or preferably fresh raspberries)

4 tablespoons of cacao powder (or cocoa powder)

Shredded coconut (for garnish)

4 cups of almond milk

4 large ripe frozen bananas

2 tablespoons of chocolate (+ more for shaving on top)

2-4 tablespoons of liquid sweetener (to taste)

Directions:

1. First, you add ingredients to blender (except sweetener and coconut).
2. After which you add sweetener to taste.
3. After that, you pour into glasses, and then sprinkle coconut and shaved chocolate on top.

Creamy Holly Nog Smoothie

INGREDIENTS:

1 cup of almond breeze

1 teaspoon of cinnamon, or to taste

1 cup of Holly nog (or preferably coconut milk nog)

2 peeled and frozen banana

1/2-1 teaspoons of ground nutmeg (to taste)

Directions:

Blend at a goal and enjoy!

Pumpkin Gingerbread Smoothie

Ingredients

½ cup of rolled oats

1 cup of pureed pumpkin

2 small frozen banana

1 teaspoon of ginger

Ice (if desired)

2 cups of almond milk (plus a bit more if necessary)

2 tablespoons of chia seeds

2 tablespoons of blackstrap molasses

2 teaspoons of cinnamon

Pinch of nutmeg

Directions:

1. First, you soak the oats, almond milk, and chia seeds for at least an hour or overnight (NOTE: This helps them digest better and it also gives the smoothie a smoother texture).
2. After which you place all ingredients into blender and blend until smooth.
3. Then you add ice if desired

Chocolate Cake Batter Smoothie

Ingredients:

2/3 cups of oats

2 teaspoons of cinnamon

2 tablespoons of carob powder/flour

4 ice cubes

2 cups of almond milk

2 frozen banana

2 teaspoons of vanilla

2 tablespoons of cashew butter (NOTE: It gives it a better taste, but other nut butters should work too)

2 tablespoons of chocolate chips

Directions:

1. First, you mix the oats and almond milk in a small bowl.
2. After which you place in fridge and let it soak for at least 1 hour to soften (NOTE: this prevents the oats from feeling too gritty in the smoothie).
3. After soaking, you add to blender along with the rest of the ingredients (except chocolate).
4. After that, you blend on high speed until smooth.
5. Then you add chocolate chips and blend on low until chunky.
6. This is when you serve and enjoy!

Note:

However, if you do not have carob powder, I suggest you try subbing 2 teaspoons of cocoa powder and 2 teaspoons of liquid sweetener.

Peppermint Patty Green Monster

Ingredients:

2-2 ½ cup of non-dairy milk (almond, soy, hemp, rice, etc.)

2-4 handfuls of spinach

2-4 tablespoons of chopped dark chocolate (for garnish)

2-3 large frozen banana (preferably, peel before freezing)

Handful of fresh mint leaves (stems removed)

¼ -1/2 teaspoon of peppermint extract (it is optional)

Directions:

1. First, you add in all of the ingredients except the chocolate into a blender and blend until smooth.
2. After which you adjust to taste and serve with a garnish of chopped dark chocolate and mint leaves.
3. Then you enjoy with a spoon.

Carrot Cake Smoothie

Ingredients:

2 cups of almond milk (or preferably coconut milk)

4 large ice cubes

1 teaspoon of pure vanilla extract

2 tablespoons of vanilla protein powder

2 large carrot (peeled and chopped into chunks)

2 large frozen banana

2 tablespoons of chia seeds (or better still ground flax)

Small pinch of cinnamon

Toppings: coconut butter, shredded Coconut, cinnamon

Directions.

1. First, you throw all ingredients into the blender, starting with the almond milk and blend until smooth.
2. Then you sprinkle on some coconut, cinnamon, and a dollop of coconut butter if you wish.

Note:

Remember this recipe works best with a high speed blender as the carrot is difficult to process.

CONCLUSION

These 22 DAY VEGAN CHALLENGE would help you Shred the Fat Instantly and keep the weight off for good. Get in shape and live a healthier lifestyle this Season taking this vegan smoothie recipes. If you follow religiously to the "22 Day Revolution" By Marco Borges and some of the recipes outlined in this book. You are going to be seeing results in 22 days, because it is proven to work.

VEGAN REV' DEIT SMOOTHIE

www.ingramcontent.com/pod-product-compliance
Lightning Source LLC
Chambersburg PA
CBHW080023130526
44591CB00036B/2589